D0934091

NAM

The Vietnam War

Disengagement and
Defeat, 1969–1975

Published by Brown Bear Books Ltd

4877 N. Circulo Bujia
Tucson, AZ 85718
USA

and

First Floor
9-17 St. Albans Place
London N1 0NX

Library of Congress Cataloging-in-Publication Data available upon request

Editorial Director: Lindsey Lowe
Managing Editor: Tim Cooke
Design Manager: Keith Davis
Designer: Lynne Lennon
Picture Manager: Sophie Mortimer
Children's Publisher: Anne O'Daly
Production Director: Alastair Gourlay

Manufactured in the United States of America

CPSIA compliance information: Batch# AG/5506

Picture Credits
Front Cover: U.S. National Archives

All photographs U.S. National Archives except:
Robert Hunt Library: 9, 16, 28, 29, 33, 35, 41, 43, 44; **TopFoto:** Picturepoint 45.

Brown Bear Books Ltd. has made every effort to contact the copyright holder. If you have any information please email smortimer@windmillbooks.co.uk

All other photographs and artworks © Brown Bear Books Ltd.

Publisher's Note
Our editors have carefully reviewed the websites that appear on page 47 to ensure that they are suitable for students. Many websites change frequently, however, and we cannot guarantee that a site's future contents will continue to meet our high standards of quality. Be advised that students should be closely supervised whenever they access the Internet.

Contents

INTRODUCTION

When U.S. troops arrived in Vietnam in March 1965, many Americans had little idea why they were going. Three years later, many were no clearer on the reason why thousands of U.S. lives had been lost fighting an enemy with whom they had no quarrel. What most Americans did know, however, was that they wanted the war to be over. In the 1968 presidential elections, they returned the Republican Richard M. Nixon, who had campaigned on a platform of bringing home the troops.

A new approach

Nixon's challenge was to end the war without conceding defeat, and to be seen to continue to support his South Vietnamese allies in their fight against Communism. He and his security adviser, Henry Kissinger, came up with a strategy called "Vietnamization." The burden of combat would be shifted to the Army of South Vietnam (ARVN). The Americans would continue to contribute financial aid, military hardware, training, and air power. Meanwhile, their troops would gradually be taken home.

▶ U.S. Marines hold a memorial service at the Quang Tri Combat Base for the 9th Marine Regiment.

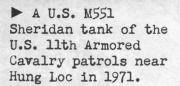

► A U.S. M551 Sheridan tank of the U.S. 11th Armored Cavalry patrols near Hung Loc in 1971.

Final withdrawal

The plan had risks. The ARVN was weak, and the U.S. withdrawal would eventually make Communist victory almost certain. Therefore Kissinger began secret peace talks with the North Vietnamese. When the Communists walked away, the U.S. launched a devastating bombing campaign that forced them back to the negotiating table. In January 1973, the Paris Peace Accords ended the fighting.

The war continued, however. Without U.S. support the South was doomed. After a pause to regroup, the North launched a final attack on the Southern capital, Saigon, in April 1975. As the last Americans in Vietnam fled by helicopter, North Vietnamese tanks rolled in and the South surrendered. After over a decade, Vietnam was finally reunited.

Chapter 1

Nixon's War

In November 1968 Americans voted in the presidential election and gave their opinion on the war in Vietnam.

Late in 1968, U.S. President Lyndon B. Johnson decided not to stand for reelection in that year's presidential election. One of the reasons was the unpopularity of the ongoing conflict in Vietnam. Johnson's decision left the way open for his Democratic Party to elect a new candidate. The obvious choice would have been Robert Kennedy, the popular brother of Johnson's predecessor, John F. Kennedy. President Kennedy had been assassinated in November 1963. But in June 1968, Robert Kennedy was also assassinated while campaigning. In his place, Hubert H. Humphrey won the nomination at the Democratic National Convention held in Chicago.

Election victory

In the minds of the U.S. electorate, Humphrey was already associated with Johnson's failed strategy in Vietnam. That gave his Republican opponent, Richard M. Nixon, the chance to present himself as an unlikely peace candidate. Nixon promised two things: he would bring "peace with honor" in Vietnam

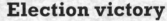
◀ Richard Nixon campaigns in the presidential election of 1968, when he avenged his defeat by John F. Kennedy in the election of 1960.

▼ U.S. infantry throw hand grenades at a VC position as they advance with an M48 Patton tank.

but also "law and order" across the United States. Civil disturbances had become more frequent across the country as antiwar feeling continued to grow. Antiwar protesters even rioted outside the Democratic Convention in Chicago. Many voters worried that the United States was heading toward anarchy. Meanwhile, "peace with honor" would be a negotiated settlement so that U.S. troops could be withdrawn from Vietnam, while still ensuring the survival of South Vietnam.

Nixon's twin strategies were popular enough to win him a narrow election victory in November 1968. On January 20, 1969,

he was sworn in as the 37th President of the United States. Henry Kissinger became the new Secretary of State and Nixon's chief advisor on foreign relations. Nixon and Kissinger took control of the war in Vietnam.

Ongoing conflict

In January, two dozen South Vietnamese cities came under artillery and rocket attack. The following month, North Vietnamese Army (NVA) and Viet Cong (VC) infantry assaults began and Saigon itself came under attack. On February 22, 1969, VC guerrilla fighters attacked U.S. bases all over South Vietnam.

The offensive began just one day after the end of the seven-day truce the VC had proclaimed for the Tet holiday. It targeted U.S. and Army of the Republic of Vietnam (ARVN) forces and installations in the Quang Nam lowlands, the An Hoa industrial complex, Tam Ky City, the Tien Phuoc Civilian Irregular Defense Group (CIDG) Camp, and Quang Ngai province.

Although they attacked Saigon, the Communists were unable to make any gains in the face of the Allies' superior artillery and airpower. On February 23, the VC and NVA attacked the Mekong Delta. For almost a week they continued to attack U.S. targets in isolated and urban regions. They were finally defeated, but at a cost of 1,140 U.S. dead.

▼ A line of U.S. M551 Sheridan tanks. Huge amounts of military hardware poured into Vietnam, at a huge cost to the U.S. taxpayer.

KEY PERSONALITY

Richard M. Nixon

Republican Nixon became the 37th president of the United States in 1968. He introduced a policy of "Vietnamization." Combat roles passed to South Vietnamese troops and U.S. troops were brought home. Nixon became very unpopular after the invasion of Cambodia in 1970. A peace agreement was signed in 1973, during his second presidential term. The next year Nixon became the only president to resign his office, after the Watergate scandal.

◀ President Nixon (right) sent Henry Cabot Lodge (left) to be chief U.S. negotiator at the Paris Peace Talks.

New approaches

Nixon's response to the increase in attacks was to authorize a new bombing campaign codenamed the MENU series. He and Kissinger authorized the secret bombing of Communist bases in neighboring Cambodia, which was also a major route for supplies being sent from North Vietnam to the South. Over the next 14 months the United States would drop more than half a million bombs on Cambodia. The bombing was kept secret because it was illegal. The United States was not at war with Cambodia.

But the Communists did not surrender. They intended to carry on fighting in the hope that growing opposition to the war in the United States would force the U.S. administration to abandon South Vietnam. Nixon and Kissinger, realizing that the enemy

was not going to surrender and that their military options were limited, started to develop a policy of "Vietnamization." This called for a gradual withdrawal of U.S. forces from Vietnam. Their roles would be filled by U.S.-trained ARVN forces that would defend their own country.

In April 1969, the number of U.S. deaths in Vietnam exceeded the total the country had suffered in the whole of the Korean War (1950–1953) with 33,629 dead. That same month, the number of U.S. troops stationed in Vietnam peaked at 543,400. U.S. intelligence meanwhile reported a new NVA build up in the A Shau Valley, which was close to the border with Laos in South Vietnam. The former U.S. commander General William Westmoreland had identified the A Shau Valley as one of the major communist

▲ UH-1 Huey helicopters
of the U.S. 101st Airborne
Division lay a smokescreen
for ground operations.

staging posts during the Tet Offensive at the beginning of 1968.

U.S. troops moved into the area to start clearing NVA troops as part of Operation Apache Snow. The operation began on May 10, 1968, and lasted for 10 days. At the head of the valley the NVA occupied fortified positions around Ap Bia Mountain, which was marked on U.S. maps as Hill 937 (its height in meters). The hill soon gained a notorious new name: Hamburger Hill. GIs said that it ground up soldiers like meat for burgers after the NVA decided to stand and fight. Despite huge losses that badly damaged morale,

KEY THEMES

Booby traps

Booby traps were an important weapon for both the Viet Cong and the NVA. They included the infamous punji stakes. These sharpened stakes of bamboo or metal were set in disguised holes so that U.S. soldiers fell in and were pierced by the spikes. If this did not kill them, they often died later from infected wounds. Other booby traps included crossbow traps, boxes of scorpions, and improvised mines made from tin cans. Between January 1965 and June 1970, booby traps caused 11 percent of U.S. fatalities. The weapons disrupted the mobility of U.S. troops, slowing advances to a snail's pace.

U.S. forces finally took the hill on May 20. After the Communist fortifications had been destroyed, however, the hill was abandoned. The NVA reoccupied it the following month.

Soon after the battle, *Life* magazine published photographs of the 242 Americans killed in just one week fighting a war that Nixon had promised he would end. Under pressure from the U.S. public, the president told General Creighton Abrams, who had succeeded General Westmoreland on July 3, 1968, as commander of U.S. forces in South Vietnam, to keep down casualties. Abrams ordered that no more major battles should be fought. Hamburger Hill was one of the last relatively large battles of the Vietnam War.

KEY MOMENT

Hamburger Hill

Hamburger Hill, fought in May 1968, was one of the most notorious battles of the war. The forested hill was defended by dug-in NVA troops. U.S. troops from 3rd Brigade, 101st Airborne were bogged down in days of fighting. A thunderstorm turned the ground to mud and morale plummeted. Eventually an attack by four battalions conquered the hill, but at a cost of 80 dead and around 400 wounded.

▶ A Vietnamese medic on Hamburger Hill signals for a helicopter to airlift casualties of the 101st Airborne Division.

Political pressure

On June 8, Nixon met the South Vietnamese president Nguyen Van Thieu on Midway Island in the Pacific Ocean. Nixon used the occasion to announce that 25,000 U.S. troops would withdraw from Vietnam by the end of July. On August 27, the 9th Infantry (minus 3rd Brigade) returned home.

The following month, the North Vietnamese leader Ho Chi Minh died. Communist forces kept up the pressure. President Thieu tried to make peace by offering elections that would include the pro-Communist National Liberation Front (NFL). Thieu's Vice President, Ky, warned that any attempt to form a coalition with the NFL

KEY THEMES

Black soldiers

Vietnam was the first war in which African Americans were fully integrated into the armed forces. Although only 11 percent of the population, they made up 12.6 percent of the soldiers who served—and 14.9 percent of casualties. Despite the danger, many found opportunities and advancement in the army that were lacking in civilian life.

would result in another military coup, similar to what had happened in the South in 1963.

In the United States, antiwar protests continued. October 15, 1969 was declared "Moratorium Day." Hundreds of thousands of protesters demonstrated against the war. In an attempt to silence the protests, Nixon went on television to promise an "orderly

▼ Troops load a casualty onto a UH-1 Huey for evacuation from the Demilitarized Zone (DMZ) in October 1969.

◄ The Americans built their airbases with landing strips in the center, so that they would be as protected as possible from outside attack.

scheduled timetable" for troop withdrawals. Still the protests continued. In Washington D.C., 250,000 antiwar protesters marched on November 15. The next day, the horrified U.S. public learned the truth about the My Lai massacre. On March 16, 1968, a U.S. patrol had murdered more than 350 unarmed civilians at the village of My Lai. The commander of the unit, Lieutenant William Calley, was charged with murder. In March 1971, he was sentenced to life imprisonment (he was paroled in November 1974).

Dual response

By the end of 1969, 475,200 U.S. military personnel remained in Vietnam, and U.S. casualties continued to rise. By the end of the year, they passed 40,000. The new year—1970—started with a new enemy offensive, as more than 100 bases came under missile fire. Nixon responded by pounding the Ho Chi Minh Trail with bombs dropped from B-52s. The NVA began a major offensive in Laos. Many people feared that Nixon was about to extend the war into Laos to support that country's anti-communist government. In February, Henry Kissinger traveled to Paris to meet the Vietnamese negotiator Le Duc Tho for secret peace talks.

On March 18, 1970, Prince Norodom Sihanouk of Cambodia was overthrown in his absence by the pro-American General Lon Nol. Vietnam's Cambodian neighbor was about to be dragged into the ground war.

Chapter 2

Laos and Cambodia

As the United States tried to limit its involvement, the war spread to Vietnam's closest neighbors.

Like Vietnam, Laos and Cambodia had once been part of the French colony of Indochina. When the French left the region in 1954, the hereditary ruler of Cambodia, Prince Norodom Sihanouk, returned to the throne. The king faced many opponents from both the right and left. In 1955, Sihanouk gave up the throne and formed his own political party. He then fixed elections to ensure that his new party won every seat in the national assembly.

Slipping into war

As neighboring Vietnam slipped toward war, Sihanouk did everything in his power to keep his country neutral. At first he courted the United States; but when U.S. troops became involved in the fighting and entered South Vietnam, he turned to China. When it became clear that the Vietnamese Communists were going to win the war, Sihanouk let them use supply routes and bases along the border,

▲ An American volunteer helps children in Laos in 1968. Laos was one of the poorest countries in the world.

▼ Helicopters of the 119th Assault Helicopter Company prepare to leave on a mission to Cambodia in May 1970.

from where it was easy to enter South Vietnam. He reasoned that the Chinese would prevent any threat to his position.

After the Communists' Tet Offensive of January 1968, however, the U.S. commander General William Westmoreland tried to get political approval to attack Communist bases in Cambodia. Realizing the potential threat, Sihanouk started to rebuild his relationship with the United States. He offered President Lyndon B. Johnson the right of "hot pursuit." U.S. forces would be allowed to follow the Viet Cong and North Vietnamese Army (NVA) into uninhabited areas of Cambodia, provided that no Cambodian civilians were hurt.

Johnson did not accept Sihanouk's offer, but it was still valid when Nixon came to power. Nixon suggested a secret "short-duration" bombing campaign against

Vietnamese strongholds in Cambodia. Sihanouk's military supplied the intelligence for the raids. The U.S. bombing carried on for 14 months but was not confined to uninhabited areas. As Cambodian casualties rose, Cambodia became more destabilized.

Coup in Cambodia

While Sihanouk was on a visit to Moscow in March 1970, his prime minister, Lon Nol, staged a bloodless coup. The coup was backed by the United States. Lon Nol's poorly trained troops attacked Vietnamese bases and massacred Vietnamese civilians who had been living peacefully in Cambodia. The NVA counterattacked, pushing the Cambodians back. From Beijing, China, Prince Sihanouk set up a government of national unity. It included the Khmer Rouge (Red Khmers).

◄ South Vietnamese Vice-President Nguyen Cao Ky (left) greets Cambodian leader Lon Nol on a visit to Phnom Penh in spring 1970.

The Khmer were the ancient people of Cambodia, and the Khmer Rouge was little more than a band of Communist guerrillas.

Backed by China and North Vietnam, Sihanouk called on the Cambodians to rise up against Lon Nol. The Khmer Rouge's tough leader, Pol Pot, distrusted both Sihanouk and the North Vietnamese. But he was a wily political operator. He knew that the peasants—the vast majority of Cambodians—listened to Sihanouk and that he needed the military strength of North Vietnam. Recruiting in areas held by the North Vietnamese, Pol Pot had built a highly trained and disciplined army by 1973.

When U.S. forces finally left Vietnam, the NVA pulled back to the border regions to prepare for the final invasion of South Vietnam. That left the Khmer Rouge in control of much of Cambodia. Pol Pot abolished money and forced the peasants to work in cooperatives. This meant he could feed his soldiers while the corrupt Lon Nol could not. Despite facing U.S. bombing and a larger number of government troops, the Khmer Rouge was unstoppable. They besieged the Cambodian capital, Phnom Penh. On April 1, 1975, Lon Nol fled the country and sought exile in the United States. On April 17, the Khmer Rouge entered the capital and began a reign of terror.

Pol Pot's Cambodia

A fanatical Communist, Pol Pot had anyone who was associated with the former government executed. He wanted to build a perfect communist society where everyone was a peasant. People could no longer work as doctors, engineers, teachers, or lawyers. Anyone who wore reading glasses was killed. Without a trained and educated workforce, the country soon fell into starvation.

Hundreds of thousands who had not been killed starved to death. It is estimated that Pol Pot and the Khmer Rouge were responsible for the deaths of two million Cambodians. In 1978, the Vietnamese invaded the country to put a stop to the killing. But since the United

▼ U.S. armor pours into Cambodia. Despite a large commitment of ground forces, the results of the invasion were disappointing.

KEY THEMES

U.S Covert Action

Congress forbade military action in Laos and Cambodia, but U.S. commanders believed the best way to destroy the North Vietnamese was through its neighbors. The CIA provided aircraft to bomb Laos and recruited Laos army officers to set up guerrilla units along the Ho Chi Minh Trail. The CIA and Special Forces also organized tribal groups to fight the Communist Pathet Lao.

States had not yet established relations with Hanoi, the Americans and much of the rest of the world condemned the invasion.

The war in Laos

When the French left Vietnam's neighbor Laos in 1954, the country was thrown into instability that would eventually result in it being dragged into the Vietnam War. Laos was split apart in 1957, when a coalition between Prince Souvanna Phouma and his half-brother Prince Souphanouvong fell apart. Souvanna and the neutralist majority of Laos turned against Souphanouvong. The United States backed Souvanna because of his anti-communist stance. The United States was worried about the so-called "domino" effect:

KEY PERSONALITY

Henry Kissinger

Henry Kissinger was an expert in security issues. In 1968, Nixon made him advisor for national security affairs. He became Secretary of State in 1973. He proposed taking a hard line with Vietnam, but when he saw the war could not be won, sought negotiations. In 1973, after months of talks, he achieved a peace settlement. He and his counterpart, North Vietnam's Le Duc Tho, shared the Nobel Peace Prize for their achievement.

▼ Soldiers of the 11th Armored Cavalry Regiment search for VC headquarters in Cambodia in May 1970.

▼ Men of the U.S. 25th Infantry Division return to base after a long-range patrol into Cambodia.

if Laos fell to the Communists, the rest of Southeast Asia would follow.

The situation grew more complicated when a series of coups saw Captain Kong Le seize power from the right-wing General Phoumi Nosavan in 1960. The United States administration was afraid that Kong Le, who was backed by the neutralists and Souvanna, might be ready to work with the Communists who, in turn, were backed by the North Vietnamese. The United States shifted its support from Souvanna and Kong Le to the right-wing General Nosavan.

At a peace conference in Geneva in 1961, it was decided that Laos was to remain neutral. The country was to be governed by a three-way government (the neutralists under Souvanna, the rightists, and the Pathet Lao, a Communist guerrilla army). By 1964, this

KEY THEMES

UH-1 Huey

In the 1950s the U.S. Army wanted a helicopter that could carry out lots of different jobs. The result was the Bell UH-1, known by its nickname of "Huey." The first Hueys arrived in Vietnam in 1963; before the end of the war, there were 5,000 in service. They could land on rough terrain, which made them perfect for the jungles and mountains of Vietnam. They served as gunships (armed with rockets and bombs), and to transport troops, for medical evacuation, and for ferrying equipment and supplies to hard-to-reach locations.

government had split and civil war broke out. The North Vietnamese wanted to increase their influence. The Ho Chi Minh Trail that kept them supplied ran through much of Laos on its way to the South. The United States wanted to sever the route. Laos was therefore inevitably drawn into the wider Vietnam War.

In an effort to try to destroy the North Vietnamese supply route, the U.S. Air Force began a secret bombing campaign in Laos, even though it had no legal power to do so. It failed to destroy the trail, but succeeded in destabilizing the country still further. From the early 1960s, the Central Intelligence Agency (CIA) and Continental Airways provided aircraft to supply anticommunist guerrillas via a network of 200 airstrips across Laos.

KEY THEMES

Tropical Warfare

One of the most dangerous enemies in Southeast Asia was the climate. The region is soaked by annual monsoon rains. Drenched in sweat and covered in leeches and insects, U.S. patrols waded through flooded paddy fields and plantations. It was so humid, cotton uniforms and leather boots rotted. Rifles such as the M16 did not work well in damp conditions and often jammed. Armored personnel carriers and tanks had only limited use in jungles and steep mountains. The army relied on helicopters to get around.

From 1965, U.S. Air Force detachments, with no visible identification, manned radio beacons in the mountains along the Vietnam border to direct U.S. bombers over North Vietnam. Special Forces ran cross-border raids, including the 1971 incursion codenamed Lam Son 719 (after a famous Vietnamese victory over the Chinese in 1419).

Air campaign

The U.S. Congress barred ground troops from entering Laos. To get round this, the U.S. government

◀ M48 tanks of the 11th Armored Cavalry Regiment patrol through the Cambodian countryside.

▲ The F-4 Phantom had formidable firepower. The U.S. Air Force used F-4s to attack the Ho Chi Minh Trail through Laos and Cambodia.

planned an air raid supported by South Vietnamese ground troops. These ARVN troops were poorly trained, understrength, and inexperienced, however.

The ARVN troops crossed the border into Laos, but when the NVA counterattacked, the ARVN suffered 50 percent casualties and had to withdraw. The U.S. Air Force's air support had been very costly, with the loss of 107 helicopters and 176 aircrew.

The failure of the mission left Laos wide open for the North Vietnamese. They used the country as a base from which to launch their Easter offensive into South Vietnam the following year. After the United States left the region in 1975, the rightists in Laos were left with no international backing. When South Vietnam and Cambodia fell to the Communists, the Pathet Lao took over Laos in a bloodless coup. Prince Souphanouvong became head of state of the Lao People's Democratic Republic, and announced the end of the 600-year-old monarchy.

Chapter 3

Vietnamization

President Nixon came up with a new war policy intended to reduce the burden on U.S. fighting forces.

Vietnamization was the name given to the new policy President Richard M. Nixon and Secretary of State Henry Kissinger adopted for Vietnam following Nixon's election victory in 1968. If it had not been clear before, it had become increasingly apparent during the first year of Nixon's presidency that the United States could not win the war in Vietnam.

Nixon's policy

Nixon had campaigned on a platform of "peace with honor." He and Kissinger were now charged with removing the United States from a war that was proving too expensive in terms of both lives lost and financial cost. In April 1969, the number of U.S. soldiers killed in the war surpassed the total for the Korean War of 1950–1953. Financially, the United States, even though it was the richest country in the world, could ill afford the $30 billion per year that the war was now costing them.

▶ Soldiers of the 41st ARVN Battalion carry out a mission in the jungle in early 1970.

◄ Instructors from the U.S. 101st Airborne Division teach ARVN instructors how to use a rappelling rope.

In March 1969, Nixon outlined a policy of "Vietnamization." The policy had two parts. Primarily, it was to be a phased withdrawal of U.S. ground troops from Vietnam. But the Americans would also give extra support to the Army of the Republic of Vietnam (ARVN) so that it could become self-sufficient. The implementation of the new policy was made more complicated in March 1970, however. The pro-United States General Lon Nol overthrew the neutral Prince Naradom Sihanouk of Cambodia in a bloodless coup. The focus of the war switched to Cambodia.

Into Cambodia

Two days after the coup, the United States began to illegally bomb and shell North Vietnamese camps in Cambodia. The bombing was a direct violation of Cambodia's neutrality. The ARVN then went into Cambodia. The North Vietnamese Army (NVA) responded by attacking U.S. positions in Vietnam.

On April 30, Nixon announced that several thousand U.S. troops supporting a Cambodian invasion had entered Cambodia's "Fishhook" area, which bordered South Vietnam. The intention was to attack the headquarters of Communist military operations in South Vietnam. Some 50,000 ARVN and 30,000

U.S. troops were involved in the series of operations that began with an ARVN invasion of the "Parrot's Beak" area on April 29.

Across Cambodia, Communists fought hard against much greater allied firepower, allowing most of the NVA to escape. Allied forces could not achieve a decisive victory. Although more than 11,000 Communists were killed, most NVA and Khmer Rouge troops escaped, only to return once the U.S. and ARVN forces left Cambodia.

▼ The result of Vietnamization: U.S. soldiers wait to travel back to the United States.

KEY PERSONALITY

Nguyen Huu Tho

Nguyen Huu Tho was a political activist in the South who had opposed French rule in Vietnam. Jailed for his activism, he escaped in the early 1960s. In 1962, he became chairman of the National Liberation Front of South Vietnam, the political wing of the Viet Cong. Tho wanted Communist rule for South Vietnam and reunification of Vietnam. When the two were reunified under Communist rule in 1976, Tho became one of two vice-presidents, and a figurehead for non-Communist South Vietnamese.

◄ This platform at the Special Forces airborne training school was used to teach ARVN personnel to parachute.

In the United States, opposition to the invasion of Cambodia turned violent. On May 4, 1970, National Guardsmen opened fire on protesting students at Kent State University in Ohio, killing four students. The same day, the Senate Foreign Relations Committee publicly accused Nixon of ignoring Congress by allowing U.S. troops to participate in the ARVN invasion of Cambodia. The next day, Nixon, aware of a possible political backlash, placed strict limits on how far into Cambodia U.S. forces were allowed to advance—19 miles (31 km)—and put a time limit of June 30 on their presence in Cambodia. To prevent a president taking such extraordinary powers in future, Congress later passed the

War Powers Act of 1973. This limited the president's ability to undertake military action without prior Congressional approval.

Fighting in Laos

Following their losses in Cambodia, the North Vietnamese concentrated their resources on Laos and the Ho Chi Minh Trail. President Thieu of South Vietnam called for an attack against the Communist build up in Laos. The invasion, codenamed Operation Lam Son 719, was to be led by the ARVN. Some 15,000 ARVN troops would advance to Tchepone in Laos to disrupt the Communist supply network. But the plan had been intercepted by the North Vietnamese. Their veteran

Vietnamization

For much of the Vietnam War, the South Vietnamese armed services had a poor reputation. This was mainly because of widespread corruption and inept leadership. As the war progressed, soldiers became better led and trained. But Vietnamization was disastrous for the Vietnamese forces, as it cut their supplies and training. Once the number of U.S. troops fell after 1973, any major Communist offensive against the South was bound to succeed.

But Lam's order to retreat came too late: the NVA's relentless attacks on the ARVN turned the retreat into a panicked rout. The U.S. Air Force once again had to come to the aid of the ARVN. Despite their heroics, half the ARVN force was killed, and 107 U.S. helicopters were lost. Although the soldiers of the ARVN had fought hard, lack of proper leadership had resulted in unnecessarily high casualties. Had it not been for U.S. intervention, the losses would have been even greater.

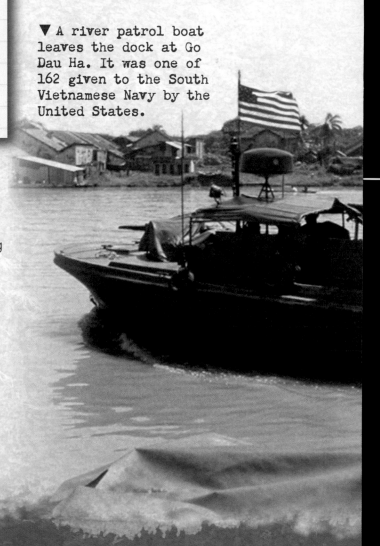

▼ A river patrol boat leaves the dock at Go Dau Ha. It was one of 162 given to the South Vietnamese Navy by the United States.

commander, General Giap, stationed almost 40,000 troops to defend the area.

On February 8, 1971, South Vietnamese troops under the command of General Hoang Xuan Lam started to advance into Laos. At this point, no U.S. troops or advisors had crossed into Laos, but that would not remain the case for long. The ARVN succeeded in taking Tchepone on March 6, but only after U.S. aircraft had provided "clandestine," or secret, air support. The ARVN forces found themselves completely exposed. To avoid a massacre, they were forced to retreat back to South Vietnam.

Reaction at home

Nixon tried unsuccessfully to present Operation Lam Son 719 as a victory. In April, to prevent the impression that the United States had completely abandoned its South Vietnamese ally, the U.S. 1st Marine Regiment launched a five-day offensive, Operation Scott Orchard, in the area west of An Hoa. The Marines met little resistance and suffered minimal casualties.

▲ South Vietnamese president Nguyen Van Thieu addresses an international conference.

At the end of April 1971, Nixon announced more troop reductions. On April 30, he welcomed home troops at Camp Pendleton, California. By the end of 1971, only 156,800 U.S. troops were left in Vietnam. Fighting was now confined to small unit combat. There were no more major engagements after Operation Imperial Lake of May 12, 1971. This was the last major U.S. Marine operation of the war, and left 305 Communists and 24 Marines dead. In the United States, people wanted the war to be over. For their part, Nixon and Kissinger were increasing their diplomatic efforts. Nixon courted both China and the Soviet Union, reasoning that if global tensions with his Communist adversaries decreased, that could only help the situation in Vietnam. Kissinger made a secret visit to China to set the scene for Nixon's historical visit there in February 1972.

The Easter Offensive

In the spring of 1972, NVA soldiers launched a massive conventional attack on South Vietnam. After years of small-scale fighting, the North Vietnamese were looking for a decisive military victory that would end the war. They sensed that the ARVN was weak and lacked the backup of the U.S. military. General Giap committed 150,000 men to his Nguyen Hue Offensive (better known in the United States as the Easter Offensive). He planned a three-pronged attack: an offensive from the Demilitarized Zone (DMZ) to take Hue, an offensive in the Central Highlands to take Kontum, and an attack from Cambodia aimed at Saigon.

The Easter Offensive failed. Despite being vastly outnumbered, the ARVN held out at Hue and were helped by massive U.S. air support. In the Highlands, constant airstrikes from U.S. B-52s broke the NVA assault and saved Kontum. Similarly, the ARVN pushed back the NVA from Saigon at An Loc. The NVA were not as good at conventional battles as they were at guerrilla warfare. For their part, the ARVN had shown that, when they were well organized and led, they could win. But the decisive factor in the failure of the Easter Offensive was U.S. airpower.

To emphasize the power of the U.S. Airforce, Nixon authorized an attack on North Vietnam, Operation Linebacker. One-half of the U.S. Strategic Air Command bomber

◀ With a grenade launcher fixed to his rifle, an ARVN soldier stands guard during an operation against the Viet Cong.

fleet—210 B-52s—bombed Hanoi and Haiphong. The bombing was the first since 1968 and was much heavier than any previous bombing.

Using "smart bombs" for the first time, Operation Linebacker destroyed most of North Vietnam's war industry. The bombing lasted for six months and left North Vietnam exhausted and battered. By now, both the Americans and the Vietnamese wanted a peaceful resolution to the conflict. The ongiong secret talks between the two sides became more important as the best chance to achieve peace.

▼ Nixon meets President Mao Zedong during his historic visit to China in February 1972.

KEY MOMENT

Nixon in China

With the war in Vietnam becoming more unpopular in the United States, Richard Nixon embarked on a highly successful public relations strategy. Relations between the United States and Communist China had been nonexistent for more than 20 years. After diplomatic meetings in 1970 and the lifting of trade and travel restrictions, Nixon sent Henry Kissinger to China for secret talks. The improved relationship between the two countries became clear during more "ping-pong" diplomacy in 1971–1972. The culmination of the diplomacy was Nixon's eight-day visit to China in February 1972, the first by a U.S. president while still in office.

Chapter 4

Toward Peace

Peace talks began in Paris but quickly ended. The United States launched new bombing raids on the North to force the Vietnamese to resume negotiations.

Operation Linebacker, the U.S. bombing campaign of April 1972, had destroyed much of Hanoi and Haiphong Harbor in North Vietnam. Meanwhile, the last major North Vietnamese offensive in South Vietnam, the Easter Offensive, had failed. In the South, the morale of U.S. soldiers was so low that military discipline had started to collapse. Some soldiers refused to go out on patrol, but they were not court-martialed.

Politically, too, the position of South Vietnam was unravelling. President Thieu had been re-elected in October 1971, but all the other candidates had boycotted the election, claiming that it had been fixed by the governing party. At the same time, the South Vietnamese Army (ARVN) found itself powerless as the U.S. Congress froze military funding to its allies.

▲ ARVN troops on M113 armored personnel carriers patrol a swampy region in the Mekong Delta, south of Saigon.

Protests at home

The withdrawal of U.S. troops continued throughout 1972, but the American public was not satisfied. There was a wave of protests across the United States in April 1972 as people rallied against the increased fighting in Southeast Asia. At the University of Maryland, 800 National Guardsmen were ordered onto the campus to keep order. Across the country, hundreds of protesting students were arrested. On April 22, 60,000 people marched in Washington, D.C., to show their hostility toward the war. It was clear that both sides wanted an end to the war and that the stalled peace talks would have to restart.

Both President Nixon and Henry Kissinger understood that the war in Vietnam would continue once the United States had left. They also realized that South Vietnam would not be able to survive on its own. Nevertheless, they believed that the time had come for America to leave the country.

Kissinger had already held negotiations with the North Vietnamese in Paris and President Nixon had unveiled an eight-point peace plan. The North Vietnamese rejected the plan in January 1972, but the South Vietnamese president, Nguyen van Thieu, saw the peace plan as clear evidence that the United States was preparing to abandon its former allies.

▼ Having just been dropped off by troop carrier, South Vietnamese Marines prepare to set off on a patrol.

KEY MOMENT

Bombing the North

As early as 1965, the United States began Operation Rolling Thunder, a program of bombing raids on North Vietnam. Pilots were not allowed to bomb civilian targets. They bombed industrial targets, railroads, bridges, and military targets, mainly in the capital, Hanoi, and the harbor of Haiphong. With the railroads destroyed, the North had problems getting food to its cities. People grew demoralized and hungry. Operation Linebacker II, launched in December 1972, was instrumental in forcing the North Vietnamese back to the negotiating table in Paris. It played a key part in the 1973 peace agreement.

Thieu's fears were confirmed in February 1972, when Nixon began his groundbreaking visit to China while Kissinger visited Moscow to prepare for a meeting with the Soviet leader Leonid Brezhnev. In fact, despite U.S. hopes, it would turn out that neither Moscow nor Beijing had any real influence with Hanoi.

Progress in Paris

After many delays at the peace talks in Paris, on October 8, 1972, the two sides made a breakthrough. Le Duc Tho, North Vietnam's chief negotiator, offered a new plan. It broadly accepted the United States' demand

▲ ARVN Airborne Division troops lay down fire against VC fighters in a street in a South Vietnamese town.

▲ South Vietnamese M113s patrol in convoy during the invasion of Laos in March 1971, codenamed Lam Son 719.

that a military cease-fire be put in place first, followed by new talks to establish a permanent political settlement.

Just before the presidential election of November 7, Kissinger announced that "peace is at hand." Nixon was reelected comfortably. But despite all the promises, the talks broke down again on December 13. South Vietnam had not been included in the discussions and President Thieu realized that the proposed peace agreement was a death sentence for his country. He refused to sign. Nixon, with the election safely behind him, felt able to stand up to Thieu, but when the

North Vietnamese also refused to return to the talks, Nixon ordered a renewed bombing of North Vietnam.

Operation Linebacker II started on December 18, 1972. For 12 days, Hanoi and Haiphong Harbor were relentlessly bombed. B-52s bombed nonstop for three days. More than 20,000 tons of bombs fell in this controversial attack, leaving a large part of

KEY THEMES

Le Duc Tho

Le Duc Tho helped found the Indochinese Communist Party in 1930. He was imprisoned twice by the French for his opposition to French rule in Vietnam. From 1955, he was a member of the Politburo of what was officially known as the Vietnam Workers' Party. Le Duc Tho is best known for his part in negotiating the ceasefire of 1973. Tho had previously served as an adviser to the North Vietnamese delegation who attended the Paris Peace conferences between 1968 and 1973.

North Vietnam's infrastructure destroyed and its cities flattened. Despite international condemnation, the Christmas bombing succeeded in bringing the North Vietnamese back to the negotiating table. Talks resumed on January 8, 1973. Meanwhile, however, ground fighting continued. The North Vietnamese Army (NVA) attacked Route 1, north of Saigon. Secretary of Defense, Melvin Laird, declared that the "Vietnamization" program was now complete, despite the fact that the ARVN was still receiving tactical help from U.S. bombers. Thieu, fearful of being

▶ A U.S. soldier opens fire on the enemy with a jeep-mounted M60 machine gun.

▶ U.S. delegates arrive at the Paris Peace Talks in 1973. The talks finalized the U.S. withdrawal.

abandoned to the Communists, demanded on January 13 that the U.S. back an invasion of the North if the peace talks broke down again.

On January 23, 1973, Nixon announced that the war was over. The Paris Peace Accords were signed four days later, on January 27. A cease-fire took effect the next day. Despite Nixon's claim to have achieved "peace with honor," however, it was clear that the Peace Accords were a sham. Kissinger had long realized that the settlement effectively represented a defeat. The best outcome the United States could hope for after all its military effort and the sacrifice of its soldiers was that a "decent interval" would pass between the final U.S. troops leaving South Vietnam and the inevitable Communist takeover of the South. Le Duc Tho proclaimed the peace talks a "victory" for the North Vietnamese.

Cease-fire in effect

From the start, both sides violated the cease-fire. A Joint Military Commission and an International Commission of Control and Supervision were established to monitor the cease-fire but, in reality, had little power to enforce it. The Saigon government started talks in Paris with the National Liberation Front (NLF), the political wing of the Communist party based in Saigon. The NLF was by now calling itself the Provisional Revolutionary Government (PRG). The two sides could not agree and the talks collapsed the following year.

Foreign ministers from 12 countries met in Paris to approve the cease-fire agreement. Canada and other Western countries granted the Hanoi government diplomatic recognition, but the United States refused to recognize Hanoi until 1974. It did, however, begin to

◄ U.S. infantry take off for an operation: "search-and-destroy" missions carried on as before.

discuss the possibility of giving the North some financial aid.

Operation Homecoming, the return of prisoners of war (POWs), began in January 1973. However, it was soon clear that not all sides were honoring the terms of the exchange. When the Saigon government was accused of keeping Communists in gaol, Thieu claimed the prisoners were "criminals," not POWs. The Americans also claimed that the North Vietnamese still held U.S. POWs.

A kind of peace

On March 29, 1973, the last U.S. combat troops left South Vietnam. "The day we have all worked for and prayed for has finally come," Nixon declared. Of the three million

KEY THEMES

Paris Peace Accords

After months of negotiation, the accords were signed in January 1973. They brought an immediate cease-fire in South and North Vietnam. All U.S. bases in the South were to be dismantled, and all foreign troops were to leave Cambodia and Laos. The renewed bombing of Hanoi and Haiphong Harbor had brought the North Vietnamese back to the negotiating table after they had quit secret talks in 1972.

Americans who had served in Vietnam, almost 58,000 had lost their lives, 1,000 were missing in action (MIA), and 150,000 were seriously wounded.

In practice, the war was far from over. The United States was still bombing Cambodia, where Khmer Rouge guerrillas threatened Phnom Penh. In Laos, the rebel Pathet Lao formed a coalition government, bringing a fragile peace after 20 years of fighting. In North Vietnam, the U.S. Navy arrived to clear mines from the ports.

In June 1973, the U.S. Congress voted to stop funds for further military action in Southeast Asia. In July, it voted to ban bombing in Cambodia. By now Nixon was distracted. He was becoming embroiled in the Watergate Scandal. When his guilt was finally exposed, he was forced to resign. On August

14, 1973, bombing in Cambodia was stopped to comply with the congressional ban.

Hanoi accused the South and the United States of not sticking to the peace plan. Meanwhile, however, it ignored the accords by making gains in the South. It was preparing for the conquest of its southern neighbor.

▼ The U.S. 327th Infantry Regiment holds a ceremony as it prepares to leave Vietnam.

Chapter 5

Communist Victory

The departure of U.S. forces left the South open to invasion by the North. The defeat of South Vietnam was inevitable.

I n January 1974, Saigon announced that there had been 57,835 fatalities since the Paris Peace Accords were signed a year earlier on January 27, 1973. In fact, the peace agreement had failed to signal an end to the fighting in Vietnam. The agreement had led to the withdrawal of the last U.S. combat troops in March 1973. But none of the leaders of the United States or South and North Vietnam were under any illusion about what was really happening.

Both President Richard M. Nixon and Secretary of State Henry Kissinger understood that the next phase of the war would inevitably lead to an eventual Communist takeover of the South. Although the South Vietnamese Army (ARVN) had held

▶ ARVN prisoners of war wait to be repatriated from Hanoi back to the South as part of the peace process.

its own during the Easter Offensive of 1972, ARVN commanders knew that they had only held off the North thanks to the help of U.S. air power. Once the U.S. military left Vietnam, the way was clear for the North Vietnamese Army (NVA) and Viet Cong (VC) to finish what they had begun.

Delayed invasion

By January 1974 the NVA was still too weak to launch a full-scale offensive into the South. When the Americans withdrew, the ARVN had more than

▲ This sign was set up outside Saigon. In fact, many U.S. veterans felt their sacrifice was forgotten all too quickly.

one million soldiers armed with the very latest U.S. weaponry. The Communists, on the other hand, had only 150,000 troops in South Vietnam and their supply lines were largely destroyed. However, the ARVN's dominance was short-lived. The NVA spent the early months of 1974 consolidating and rebuilding their divisions south of the Demilitarized Zone (DMZ).

Standing alone

The South Vietnamese President Thieu had not really believed that the United States would completely abandon South Vietnam to the Communists. He reasoned that so much blood had been spilled and so much money spent that the Americans would stay.

KEY THEMES

B-52s

The Boeing B-52 was the first Stratofortress bomber to participate in combat. It first hit Viet Cong strongholds north of Saigon on June 18, 1965, during Operation Arc Light. By the end of the year, Arc Light had flown more than 1,500 sorties against enemy troops, bases, and supply dumps. At the end of the war the B-52s proved their worth in the bombing of North Vietnam in the two Linebacker operations, which forced the Communists back to the peace talks.

But when the U.S. Congress passed the War Powers Resolution in 1973, it meant that Nixon or any future president would need Congressional approval for any troop deployment overseas. That effectively ended any hope of South Vietnam receiving any further military aid from the United States.

The situation worsened when President Nixon resigned on August 9, 1974, rather than face impeachment over the Watergate scandal. Nixon was accused of having covered up a break-in by Democratic Party supporters into a Republican Party office. Nixon had been South Vietnam's strongest supporter within the administration. His replacement, Vice-President Gerald Ford, had not won an election and had no real mandate to govern. He was not prepared to take the risk of asking Congress to supply U.S. troops to return to Vietnam.

◄ The so-called "Boat People" fled from Vietnam on any sort of vessel they could find. Many drowned when their boats sank.

▲ Khmer Rouge guerillas in Cambodia. After the Vietnam War, the Vietnamese eventually invaded to topple the tyrannical regime.

Continued aid

Although the South Vietnamese regime was technically on its own, the United States still sent $2.3 billion in aid in 1973. The following year, the sum was cut to $1.1 billion dollars. As a result, the South Vietnamese economy collapsed. Poverty spread as inflation of over 200 percent caused prices to rocket. The misery brought by the economic collapse left many South Vietnamese with little reason to try to defend their nation against Communists who promised them a better future.

The reduction in U.S. aid meant that the South could no longer cover the cost of running the vast ARVN. It could not afford to fuel and maintain its modern trucks, jets, and

helicopters: in effect, the ARVN could no longer fight anybody.

The NVA and Viet Cong were poised to take advantage. By the end of 1974, the North Vietnamese had recovered from their losses of 1972. They were armed with the latest Soviet weapons and ready to test their capabilities. On December 26, 1974, the NVA 7th division took Dong Xoai. On January 6, 1975, it took Phuoc Long Province. The attack contravened the Paris Peace Accords, but when President Thieu asked the United

▲ U.S. Marines on an amphibious assault ship prepare ammunition before flying into Saigon on an evacuation mission.

States for help, no American aid came. If the Americans would not fight to enforce the accords, no-one would.

The mood in Hanoi was triumphant. The North Vietnamese prepared to launch an all-out offensive against the South, which they knew would finally end the war.

Beginning of the end

On March 1, 1975, the NVA launched an offensive in the Central Highlands. Five divisions attacked and the ARVN quickly found themselves outnumbered and surrounded. Within a week the town had fallen to the NVA. The resulting South Vietnamese withdrawal was a catastrophe. President Thieu's order to retreat to the coastal city of Tuy Hoa led to 200,000 soldiers and civilians trying to flee down one main road. As the road became jammed,

KEY THEMES

Last Flight

One of the lasting images of the Vietnam War is the evacuation of people by helicopter from the roof of the U.S. Embassy in Saigon. The Americans planned to rescue some 200,000 Vietnamese allies, but the fall of Saigon was so quick there was no time. On April 20, 1973, evacuations began but soon descended into chaos as the air base came under sniper fire. Helicopters started to pluck people from roofs across the city to fly them to waiting aircraft carriers. Crowds outside the U.S. Embassy panicked as the North Vietnamese approached. Some 2,100 people were rescued from the Embassy roof.

artillery shells rained down on the trapped victims. Nearly 100,000 people died or were captured by the NVA. Another NVA offensive of 100,000 soldiers attacked the northern region of South Vietnam. Nearly two million refugees, including soldiers who had removed their uniforms to blend in with civilians, fled to the coastal city of Danang. It soon fell to the NVA, followed by Hue, the third-largest city in South Vietnam.

Final offensive

By early April, just five weeks into their campaign, the NVA had made gains far beyond their expectations. Twelve provinces and more than eight million people were under North Vietnamese control. The South Vietnamese had lost their best fighting units, over a third of their men, and almost half their weapons. The final push to Saigon was underway. The North Vietnamese wanted to capture the city before the monsoon rains started, so they quickly launched the Ho Chi Minh offensive.

In early April the ARVN 18th Division defended the critical road junction of Xuan Loc as 40,000 NVA attacked. After what proved the single most costly battle of the

▼ An NVA tank enters the gates of the Presidential Palace in Saigon after the fall of the city.

war, Xuan Loc finally fell on April 21. The route to Saigon was now open. President Thieu resigned and fled the country, blaming its imminent defeat on its abandonment by the United States.

Evacuation and defeat

On April 25, the NVA attacked Saigon. At the same time, the United States started a belated evacuation program of U.S. citizens and South Vietnamese who had been an integral part of the war effort. The events

▼ The NVA and their VC allies had proved a determined enemy who ultimately defeated the world's leading superpower.

KEY THEMES
. . . .

The Boat People

The end of the war did not end the suffering of the Vietnamese. As the Communists took over, many South Vietnamese feared punishment. Many were executed or sent to prison. Others fled by cramming onto makeshift vessels. Up to 1.5 million may have set sail. Many did not make it: some 50,000 to 200,000 died from drowning or were kidnapped and sold into slavery. Those who made it to safety became refugees. The United States took 823,000 boat people.

◄ Marines stand guard as a helicopter leaves the U.S. Embassy during the evacuations.

On April 30, two U.S. Marines guarding Saigon's airport were killed. They were the last Americans to die in Vietnam. At dawn that same day, the last Marine guards left the U.S. Embassy. Hours later, the building was ransacked by looters. At noon, a group of NVA tanks crashed through the gates of the Presidential Palace, the last symbol of South Vietnamese authority.

Inside the palace, the last president of South Vietnam, General Minh, was waiting to surrender to the North Vietnamese victors. The NVA officer who accepted the surrender was Colonel Bui Tin, who also worked as a reporter for the NVA newspaper. When Tin entered the room, Minh is said to have told him he had been waiting to transfer power to him. Tin allegedly replied, "There is no question of your transferring power. Your power has crumbled. You cannot give up what you do not have."

Cost of the war

The Vietnam War was finally over. It had lasted 15 years. Nearly one million NVA and Viet Cong troops had been killed in the fight for the South, while a quarter of a million South Vietnamese soldiers had died trying to resist them. And hundreds of thousands of civilians had also lost their lives.

after the fall of Hue suggested that the North Vietnamese would show little mercy to those who had fought for the South.

Operation Frequent Wind used ships and aircraft to evacuate thousands in an increasingly desperate mission. As the NVA's hold on Saigon tightened, U.S. forces had to stop using airplanes and ships and rely entirely on helicopter evacuations from the city.

GLOSSARY

accords Agreements reached after an official process of negotiations.

assassination A murder carried out for political reasons.

clandestine Something that is carried out in secret.

coup The sudden or violent overthrow and replacement of a goverment by a small group.

delta A large triangular-shaped area formed at the mouth of a river and often cut by many water channels.

deploy To distribute military forces ready for action.

dictator A ruler who is able to do entirely what he or she wishes.

guerrilla Someone who fights by irregular means such as ambush, sabotage, and assassination.

Indochina A peninsula in Southeast Asia that includes Myanmar, Cambodia, Laos, Thailand, and Vietnam; also the French colony that formerly occupied much of the region.

intelligence Information about the enemy, gathered by patrolling, reconnaissance, or espionage.

morale The fighting spirit of an individual or a group, and how much they believe in victory.

negotiations Official talks aiming to achieve a compromise between two sides.

rappelling Using a rope to slide quickly to the ground from a height such as a cliff-top or a hovering helicopter.

reconnaissance Gathering information about the enemy by patrols and other direct means.

sabotage Destroying infrastructure to hamper the operations of the enemy.

strategic Something that is related to the overall course of a conflict, rather than to a short-term victory in a single battle.

Viet Cong A guerrilla member of the Vietnamese Communist movement.

Vietnamization A U.S. policy to ensure the fighting in Vietnam was done increasingly by South Vietnamese rather than by U.S. forces.

FURTHER RESOURCES

Books

Britton, Tamara L. *Richard Nixon: 37th President of the United States* (United States Presidents). Abdo Publishing Company, 2009.

DiConsiglio, John. *Vietnam: The Bloodbath at Hamburger Hill* (24/7: Goes to War). Franklin Watts, 2009.

Gitlin, Marty. *U.S. Involvement in Vietnam* (Essential Events). Abdo Publishing Company, 2010.

Kent, Deborah. *The Vietnam War: From Da Nang to Saigon* (The United States at War). Enslow Publishing Inc, 2011.

McNeese, Tim. *The Cold War and Postwar America, 1946–1963*. Chelsea House Publications, 2010.

O'Connell, Kim A. *Primary Source Accounts of the Vietnam War* (America's Wars through Primary Sources). Myreportlinks.com, 2006.

Tougas, Shelley. *Weapons, Gear, and Uniforms of the Vietnam War* (Edge Books). Capstone Press, 2012.

The Vietnam War (Perspectives on Modern World History). Greenhaven Press, 2011.

Wiest, Andrew. *The Vietnam War* (Essential Histories: War and Conflict in Modern Times). Rosen Publishing Group, 2008.

Websites

http://www.pbs.org/wgbh/amex/vietnam/
Online companion to the PBS series *Vietnam: A Television History*.

www.history.com/topics/vietnam-war
History.com page of links about the Vietnam War.

http://www.spartacus.schoolnet.co.uk/vietnam.htm
Spartacus Educational page with links to biographies and other articles.

INDEX